British Columbia Ecoregions

- ■ Boreal Cordillera
- ■ Western Cordillera
- ■ Marine West Coast Forest
- ☐ Taiga Plain
- ■ Boreal Plain
- ☐ Cold Deserts

1. Liard River Hotsprings Provincial Park
2. Stone Mountain Provincial Park
3. Pink Mountain
4. Tabor Mountain
5. Mount Robson Provincial Park
6. Bowron Lake Provincial Park
7. Kootenay National Park
8. Kokanee Creek Provincial Park
9. Yoho National Park
10. Mount Revelstoke National Park
11. Shannon Falls Provincial Park
12. Roderick Haig-Brown Provincial Park
13. Kalamalka Lake Provincial Park
14. Okanagan Falls Provincial Park
15. Manning Provincial Park
16. Coquihalla Canyon Provincial Park
17. French Beach Provincial Park
18. Pacific Rim National Park
19. George C. Reifel Migratory Bird Sanctuary
20. Strathcona Provincial Park
21. Blackfish Sound/ Johnstone Strait
22. South Moresby Island/ Gwaii Haanas National Park Preserve
23. Royal BC Museum
24. The Beaty Biodiversity Museum
25. The Vancouver Aquarium

A POCKET NATURALIST® GUIDE

BRITISH COLUMBIA WILDLIFE

A Folding Pocket Guide to Familiar Animals

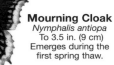

BRITISH COLUMBIA WILDLIFE – A Folding Pocket Guide to Familiar Animals

WATERFORD PRESS

INVERTEBRATES

Aggregate Anemone
Anthopleura elegantissima
To 20 in. (50 cm)

Frilled Anemone
Metridium senile
To 18 in. (45 cm)

Giant Green Anemone
Anthopleura xanthogrammica
To 12 in. (30 cm)

Bat Star
Patiria miniata
To 8 in. (20 cm)
May be red-brown to reddish.

Ochre Sea Star
Pisaster ochraceus
To 20 in. (50 cm)
May be red, purple, orange or brown.

Giant Western Nassa
Nassarius fossatus
To 2 in. (5 cm)

Blue Mussel
Mytilus edulis
To 4 in. (10 cm)
Grows attached to pilings and other marine objects.

Giant Pacific Scallop
Patinopecten caurinus
To 10 in. (25 cm)

Giant Pacific Oyster
Crassostrea gigas
To 12 in. (30 cm)

Red Crab
Cancer productus
To 6 in. (15 cm)

Pacific Littleneck Clam
Protothaca staminea
To 3 in. (8 cm)

Purple Shore Crab
Hemigrapsus nudus
To 2.5 in. (6 cm)

Barnacle
Balanus spp.
To 3 in. (8 cm)
Often grows in clusters attached to rocks and piers.

Dungeness Crab
Cancer magister
To 9 in. (23 cm)

Banana Slug
Ariolimax columbianus
To 10 in. (25 cm)

European Slug
Arion ater
To 6 in. (15 cm)

INVERTEBRATES

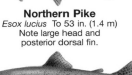

Yellow Jacket
Vespula spp.
To .5 in. (1.3 cm)
Black and yellow with a banded abdomen. Protects itself with a stinger.

Mosquito larvae are found floating on the water's surface.

Mosquito
Family Culicidae
To .5 in. (1.3 cm)
Slender insect has a thin, blood-sucking beak.

Bumble Bee
Bombus spp.
To 1 in. (3 cm)
Stout, furry bee is large and noisy.

Crane Fly
Tipula spp.
To 2.5 in. (6 cm)
Slender fly has a long abdomen and long legs.

Green Darner
Anax junius
To 3 in. (8 cm)
Has a bright green thorax and a blue body. Rests with its wings open.

Ladybug Beetle
Family Coccinellidae
To 5 in. (1.3 cm)
Red wing covers are black-spotted.

Garden Spider
Family Araneidae
To 1.25 in. (3.2 cm)
Dark spider with white spots builds concentric webs suspended vertically from vegetation, fences, etc.

American Cockroach
Periplaneta americana
To 2 in. (5 cm)

Ground Beetle
Family Carabidae
To 1.5 in. (4 cm)

Caddisfly
Order Trichoptera
To 1 in. (3 cm)
Moth-like, brown insect has hairy wings and long, thin antennae.

Tiger Swallowtail
Papilio glaucus
To 6 in. (15 cm)
Note "tailed" hindwings.

Monarch
Danaus plexippus
To 4 in. (10 cm)
Note rows of white spots on edges of wings. Millions migrate between the U.S. and the forests of central Mexico each year.

Spring Azure
Celastrina ladon
To 1.25 in. (3.2 cm)
One of the earliest spring butterflies.

Cabbage White
Pieris rapae
To 2 in. (5 cm)
One of the most common butterflies. Larvae feed on cabbage leaves and wild mustards.

Mourning Cloak
Nymphalis antiopa
To 3.5 in. (9 cm)
Emerges during the first spring thaw.

FISHES

Northern Pike
Esox lucius To 4.5 ft. (1.4 m)
Note large head and posterior dorsal fin.

Cutthroat Trout
Oncorhynchus clarkii To 39 in. (98 cm)
Told by red mark near throat.

Rainbow Trout
Oncorhynchus mykiss To 44 in. (1.1 m)
Note reddish side stripe.

Brook Trout
Salvelinus fontinalis To 28 in. (70 cm)
Reddish side spots have blue halos.

Dolly Varden
Salvelinus malma To 25 in. (63 cm)
Green to brown above, covered with small pink to yellow spots.

Lake Whitefish
Coregonus clupeaformis
To 30 in. (75 cm)
Note concave forehead.

Lake Trout
Salvelinus namaycush To 4 ft. (1.2 m)
Dark fish is covered in light spots. Tail is deeply forked.

Largemouth Bass
Micropterus salmoides To 40 in. (1 m)
Jaw joint extends beyond the eye.

Chinook (King) Salmon
Oncorhynchus tshawytscha
To 5 ft. (1.5 m)
Has dark spots on back and tail. Gums are black at tooth base.

Chum (Dog) Salmon
Oncorhynchus keta To 40 in. (1 m)
Breeding male has blotchy red sides.
Salmon are the provincial fish of B.C.

Coho (Silver) Salmon
Oncorhynchus kisutch To 40 in. (1 m)
Breeding male has red side stripes.

Sockeye (Red) Salmon
Oncorhynchus nerka To 33 in. (83 cm)
Red breeding male has hooked jaws and a green head.

Steelhead
Oncorhynchus mykiss To 45 in. (1.1 m)
Sea-run version of rainbow trout is silvery.

Pink (Humpbacked) Salmon
Oncorhynchus gorbuscha
To 30 in. (75 cm)
Breeding male has strongly humped back.

REPTILES & AMPHIBIANS

Painted Turtle
Chrysemys picta
To 10 in. (25 cm)
Note red marks on outer edge of shell.

Northern Alligator Lizard
Elgaria coerulea To 12 in. (30 cm)

Western Skink
Plestiodon skiltonianus To 9 in. (23 cm)
Has 4 light body stripes.

Rough-skinned Newt
Taricha granulosa
To 8 in. (20 cm)
Skin is warty.

Northwestern Salamander
Ambystoma gracile To 9 in. (23 cm)
Brownish, with large swellings behind its eyes.

Wood Frog
Lithobates sylvaticus
To 3 in. (8 cm)
Note dark mask. Staccato call is duck-like.

Long-toed Salamander
Ambystoma macrodactylum To 7 in. (18 cm)
Has line of light blotches down back.

Pacific Treefrog
Pseudacris regilla
To 2 in. (5 cm)
Color ranges from brown to green. Note dark eye stripe. Call is 2-part — *kreck-ek* — with the last syllable rising.

Spotted Frog
Rana pretiosa
To 4 in. (10 cm)
Call is a series of short croaks.

Boreal Toad
Anaxyrus boreas
To 4 in. (10 cm)
Males have a soft, clucking call.

Western Terrestrial Garter Snake
Thamnophis elegans
To 42 in. (1 m)
Has a defined back stripe and dark side spots.

Common Garter Snake
Thamnophis sirtalis
To 4 ft. (1.2 m)
Has yellowish back and side stripes. Color and pattern are variable.

Gopher Snake
Pituophis catenifer To 8 ft. (2.4 m)
Note pointed snout.

Northern Pacific Rattlesnake
Crotalus oreganus oreganus
To 5 ft. (1.5 m)
Note dark blotches on back and spade-shaped head.

Common Loon
Gavia immer To 3 ft. (90 cm)
Winter / Summer

Western Grebe
Aechmophorus occidentalis
To 25 in. (63 cm)

Trumpeter Swan
Cygnus buccinator
To 6 ft. (1.8 m)
Note stout black bill.

American Coot
Fulica americana To 16 in. (40 cm)

Canada Goose
Branta canadensis
To 45 in. (1.14 m)

Green-winged Teal
Anas crecca To 15 in. (38 cm)

Northern Pintail
Anas acuta To 30 in. (75 cm)

Common Merganser
Mergus merganser To 27 in. (68 cm)
Note slender profile and thin red bill.

Common Goldeneye
Bucephala clangula To 18 in. (45 cm)

American Wigeon
Mareca americana To 23 in. (58 cm)

Mallard
Anas platyrhynchos To 28 in. (70 cm)

Greater Scaup
Aythya marila To 20 in. (50 cm)
Note rounded head.

Double-crested Cormorant
Phalacrocorax auritus
To 3 ft. (90 cm)

Great Blue Heron
Ardea herodias
To 4.5 ft. (1.4 m)

Spotted Sandpiper
Actitis macularius
To 8 in. (20 cm)
Breast is spotted.

Herring Gull
Larus argentatus
To 26 in. (65 cm)
Legs are pinkish.

Killdeer
Charadrius vociferus
To 6 in. (15 cm)
Note two breast bands.

Belted Kingfisher
Megaceryle alcyon
To 14 in. (35 cm)

Rufous Hummingbird
Selasphorus rufus
To 3.5 in. (9 cm)

Rock Pigeon
Columba livia
To 13 in. (33 cm)

Red-tailed Hawk
Buteo jamaicensis
To 25 in. (63 cm)

Ruffed Grouse
Bonasa umbellus
To 19 in. (48 cm)
Note black tail band.

Bald Eagle
Haliaeetus leucocephalus
To 40 in. (1 m)

Northern Harrier
Circus hudsonius
To 22 in. (55 cm)
Note V-shaped flight profile and white rump.

Osprey
Pandion haliaetus
To 2 ft. (60 cm)

American Kestrel
Falco sparverius
To 12 in. (30 cm)

Great Horned Owl
Bubo virginianus
To 25 in. (63 cm)
Call is a resonant –
hoo-HOO-hoooo.

Downy Woodpecker
Dryobates pubescens
To 6 in. (15 cm)
The similar hairy woodpecker is larger and has a longer bill.

Northern Flicker
Colaptes auratus
To 13 in. (33 cm)
Wing and tail linings are red.

Barn Swallow
Hirundo rustica
To 8 in. (20 cm)
Note deeply forked tail.

Black-capped Chickadee
Poecile atricapillus
To 6 in. (15 cm)

American Robin
Turdus migratorius
To 11 in. (28 cm)

Common Raven
Corvus corax
To 27 in. (68 cm)
Call is a hoarse croak.

European Starling
Sturnus vulgaris
To 8 in. (20 cm)

American Crow
Corvus brachyrhynchos
To 22 in. (55 cm)
Call is a distinct – caw.

American Goldfinch
Spinus tristis
To 5 in. (13 cm)

Purple Finch
Haemorhous purpureus
To 6 in. (15 cm)

Cedar Waxwing
Bombycilla cedrorum
To 7 in. (18 cm)
Red wing marks look like waxy droplets.

Song Sparrow
Melospiza melodia
To 7 in. (18 cm)

Chipping Sparrow
Spizella passerina
To 5 in. (13 cm)
Note chestnut cap.

House Sparrow
Passer domesticus
To 6 in. (15 cm)

Canada Jay
Perisoreus canadensis
To 14 in. (35 cm)

Spotted Towhee
Pipilo maculatus
To 9 in. (23 cm)

Steller's Jay
Cyanocitta stelleri
To 14 in. (35 cm)
Provincial bird of B.C.

Dark-eyed Junco
Junco hyemalis To 7 in. (18 cm)
Note dark hood and light bill.
Oregon Race / Slate-colored Race

Virginia Opossum
Didelphis virginiana
To 40 in. (1 m)
Note long fur and naked tail.

Masked Shrew
Sorex cinereus
To 4.5 in. (11.5 cm)
Note pointed nose.

Little Brown Bat
Myotis lucifugus
To 3.5 in. (9 cm)

American Pika
Ochotona princeps
To 9 in. (23 cm)
Inhabits rock piles in mountainous areas.

Red Squirrel
Tamiasciurus hudsonicus
To 14 in. (35 cm)

Snowshoe Hare
Lepus americanus
To 20 in. (50 cm)
Coat is white in winter.

Northern Flying Squirrel
Glaucomys sabrinus
To 14 in. (35 cm)

Columbian Ground Squirrel
Urocitellus columbianus
To 16 in. (40 cm)
Grayish above and red-brown below.

Western Gray Squirrel
Sciurus griseus
To 23 in. (58 cm)

Deer Mouse
Peromyscus maniculatus
To 8 in. (20 cm)
Distinguished by its white undersides and hairy tail.

Chipmunk
Neotamias spp.
To 12 in. (30 cm)
Note white stripes on side and face.

Norway Rat
Rattus norvegicus
To 18 in. (45 cm)
Brown to gray rodent has a naked tail.

Red-backed Vole
Clethrionomys spp.
To 6 in. (15 cm)

Common Muskrat
Ondatra zibethicus
To 2 ft. (60 cm)
Aquatic rodent has a naked, scaly tail.

Woodrat
Neotoma spp.
To 18 in. (45 cm)

Hoary Marmot
Marmota caligata To 32 in. (80 cm)

Common Porcupine
Erethizon dorsatum To 3 ft. (90 cm)

Striped Skunk
Mephitis mephitis
To 32 in. (80 cm)
Rope-like tail is black-tipped.

Common Raccoon
Procyon lotor To 40 in. (1 m)

American Beaver
Castor canadensis
To 4 ft. (1.2 m)

Sea Otter
Enhydra lutris To 6 ft. (1.8 m)

American Badger
Taxidea taxus To 35 in. (88 cm)

Mink
Neovison vison
To 28 in. (70 cm)

Short-tailed Weasel
Mustela erminea
To 14 in. (35 cm)

Coyote
Canis latrans To 52 in. (1.3 m)

Red Fox
Vulpes vulpes To 40 in. (1 m)
Note white-tipped tail.

Mountain Lion
Puma concolor To 9 ft. (2.7 m)

Gray Wolf
Canis lupus To 6.5 ft. (2 m)
Coat color is usually gray, but black, white and mottled variants exist.

Lynx
Lynx lynx To 42 in. (1.06 m)

Mountain Goat
Oreamnos americanus To 6 ft. (1.8 m)
Note long white coat and black horns.

Mule Deer
Odocoileus hemionus
To 7.5 ft. (2.3 m)
Rope-like tail is black-tipped.

White-tailed Deer
Odocoileus virginianus
To 7 ft. (2.1 m)
Fluffy tail is white below and held aloft when running.

Elk
Cervus canadensis
To 10 ft. (3 m)

Bighorn Sheep
Ovis canadensis
To 6 ft. (1.8 m)

Grizzly Bear
Ursus arctos
To 7 ft. (2.1 m)
Large brownish bear has a prominent shoulder hump and a "dished" face.

Moose
Alces alces
To 10 ft. (3 m)

Black Bear
Ursus americanus
To 6 ft. (1.8 m)
Coat may be black, brown, cinnamon or blonde. The rare white "spirit bear" is the provincial mammal of B.C.

Northern Sea Lion
Eumetopias jubatus
To 10.5 ft. (3.2 m)
Males have hairy necks.

Harbor Seal
Phoca vitulina
To 6 ft. (1.8 m)

Killer Whale
Orcinus orca To 30 ft. (9 m)

Dall's Porpoise
Phocoenoides dalli
To 7 ft. (2.1 m)

Humpback Whale
Megaptera novaeangliae
To 50 ft. (15 m)
Long flippers have scalloped edges.